C000131176

SAM HOLCROFT

Sam Holcroft's other plays include *Rules for Living* at the
National Theatre; *Edgar & Annabel*, part of the *Double Feature*
season in the Paintframe at the National Theatre; *Dancing
Bears*, part of the *Charged* season for Clean Break at Soho
Theatre and Latitude Festival; *While You Lie* at the Traverse,
Edinburgh; *Pink*, part of the *Women, Power and Politics* season
at the Tricycle; *Vanya*, adapted from Chekhov, at The Gate; and
Cockroach, co-produced by the National Theatre of Scotland
and the Traverse (nominated for Best New Play 2008, by the
Critics' Awards for Theatre in Scotland and shortlisted for the
John Whiting Award, 2009). In 2013, Sam wrote *The House
Taken Over*, a libretto for opera, adapted from Cortázar, for the
Festival d'Aix-en-Provence and Académie Européenne de
Musique. Sam received the Tom Erhardt Award in 2009, was
the Pearson Writer-in-Residence at the Traverse Theatre, 2009–
10, and the Writer-in-Residence at the National Theatre Studio
from 2013–14. In 2014, Sam received a Windham Campbell
Prize for Literature in the drama category.

Other Titles in this Series

Mike Bartlett
BULL
GAME
AN INTERVENTION
KING CHARLES III
WILD

Deborah Bruce
THE DISTANCE
GODCHILD
THE HOUSE THEY GREW UP IN
SAME

Jez Butterworth
THE FERRYMAN
JERUSALEM
JEZ BUTTERWORTH PLAYS: ONE
MOJO
THE NIGHT HERON
PARLOUR SONG
THE RIVER
THE WINTERLING

Caryl Churchill
BLUE HEART
CHURCHILL PLAYS: THREE
CHURCHILL PLAYS: FOUR
CHURCHILL: SHORTS
CLOUD NINE
DING DONG THE WICKED
A DREAM PLAY *after* Strindberg
DRUNK ENOUGH TO SAY
    I LOVE YOU?
ESCAPED ALONE
FAR AWAY
HERE WE GO
HOTEL
ICECREAM
LIGHT SHINING IN
    BUCKINGHAMSHIRE
LOVE AND INFORMATION
MAD FOREST
A NUMBER
PIGS AND DOGS
SEVEN JEWISH CHILDREN
THE SKRIKER
THIS IS A CHAIR
THYESTES *after* Seneca
TRAPS

Elinor Cook
THE GIRL'S GUIDE TO SAVING
    THE WORLD
IMAGE OF AN UNKNOWN
    YOUNG WOMAN
OUT OF LOVE
PILGRIMS

debbie tucker green
BORN BAD
DIRTY BUTTERFLY
HANG
NUT
A PROFOUNDLY AFFECTIONATE,
    PASSIONATE DEVOTION TO
    SOMEONE (– *NOUN*)
RANDOM
STONING MARY
TRADE & GENERATIONS
TRUTH AND RECONCILIATION

Alan Harris
HOW MY LIGHT IS SPENT
LOVE, LIES AND TAXIDERMY
SUGAR BABY

Sam Holcroft
COCKROACH
DANCING BEARS
EDGAR & ANNABEL
PINK
RULES FOR LIVING
WHILE YOU LIE

Vicky Jones
THE ONE
TOUCH

Anna Jordan
CHICKEN SHOP
FREAK
YEN

Lucy Kirkwood
BEAUTY AND THE BEAST
    with Katie Mitchell
BLOODY WIMMIN
THE CHILDREN
CHIMERICA
HEDDA *after* Ibsen
IT FELT EMPTY WHEN THE
    HEART WENT AT FIRST BUT
    IT IS ALRIGHT NOW
LUCY KIRKWOOD PLAYS: ONE
MOSQUITOES
NSFW
TINDERBOX

James Rushbrooke
TOMCAT

Sam Steiner
LEMONS LEMONS LEMONS
    LEMONS LEMONS

Jack Thorne
2ND MAY 1997
BUNNY
BURYING YOUR BROTHER IN
    THE PAVEMENT
HOPE
JACK THORNE PLAYS: ONE
LET THE RIGHT ONE IN
    after John Ajvide Lindqvist
MYDIDAE
THE SOLID LIFE OF SUGAR WATER
STACY & FANNY AND FAGGOT
WHEN YOU CURE ME
WOYZECK
    after Büchner

Phoebe Waller-Bridge
FLEABAG

Tom Wells
BROKEN BISCUITS
FOLK
JUMPERS FOR GOALPOSTS
THE KITCHEN SINK
ME, AS A PENGUIN

Monsay Whitney
BOX CLEVER

Sam Holcroft

THE WARDROBE

NICK HERN BOOKS
London
www.nickhernbooks.co.uk

A Nick Hern Book

The Wardrobe first published as a single edition paperback in Great Britain in 2014 by Nick Hern Books Limited, The Glasshouse, 49a Goldhawk Road, London W12 8QP

Reprinted 2017

The Wardrobe copyright © 2014 Sam Holcroft

Sam Holcroft has asserted her right to be identified as the author of this work

Cover image © Shutterstock.com/draconus

Designed and typeset by Nick Hern Books, London
Printed in Great Britain by Mimeo Ltd, Cambridgeshire PE29 6XX

A CIP catalogue record for this book is available from the British Library

ISBN   978 1 84842 409 8

CAUTION   All rights whatsoever in this play are strictly reserved. Requests to reproduce the text in whole or in part should be addressed to the publisher.

Amateur Performing Rights   Applications for performance, including readings and excerpts, by amateurs in the English language throughout the world should be addressed to the Performing Rights Manager, Nick Hern Books, The Glasshouse, 49a Goldhawk Road, London W12 8QP, *email* rights@nickhernbooks.co.uk, except as follows:

Australia: Dominie Drama, 8 Cross Street, Brookvale 2100, *tel* (2) 9938 8686, *fax* (2) 9938 8695, *email* drama@dominie.com.au

New Zealand: Play Bureau, PO Box 9013, St Clair, Dunedin 9047, *tel* (3) 455 9959, *email* info@playbureau.com

South Africa: DALRO (pty) Ltd, PO Box 31627, 2017 Braamfontein, *tel* (11) 712 8000, *fax* (11) 403 9094, *email* theatricals@dalro.co.za

USA and Canada: Casarotto Ramsay and Associates Ltd, see details below

Professional Performing Rights   Applications for performance by professionals in any medium and in any language throughout the world (including by stock companies in the USA and Canada) should be addressed to Casarotto Ramsay and Associates Ltd, Waverley House, 7–12 Noel Street, London W1F 8GQ, *fax* +44 (0)20 7287 9128, *email* agents@casarotto.co.uk

No performance of any kind may be given unless a licence has been obtained. Applications should be made before rehearsals begin. Publication of this play does not necessarily indicate its availability for amateur performance.

Woodland
CARBON
www.woodlandcarbon.co.uk
NICK HERN BOOKS
Printed on Carbon Captured paper

The Wardrobe was commissioned as part of the 2014 National Theatre Connections Festival and premiered by youth theatres across the UK, including a performance at the National Theatre in July 2014.

Each year the National Theatre asks ten writers to create new plays to be performed by young theatre companies all over the country. From Scotland to Cornwall and Northern Ireland to Norfolk, Connections celebrates great new writing for the stage – and the energy, commitment and talent of young theatremakers.

www.nationaltheatre.org.uk/connections

Characters
in order of appearance

ELIZABETH, *eighteen*
CECILY, *sixteen*

BENJAMIN, *seventeen*
DANIEL, *thirteen*

HENRY, *thirteen*
MATHILDA, *sixteen*
TOBIAS, *eighteen*
CARYL, *sixteen*

ANNE, *seventeen*
MARY, *sixteen*
SARAH, *sixteen*

ONE, *seventeen*
TWO, *fifteen*

DIDO, *thirteen*

WILLIAM, *sixteen*
JAFFREY, *sixteen*

MARTIN, *sixteen*
ROBERT, *nine*

TOM, *fifteen*
ARCHIE, *sixteen*
HUGO, *fifteen*
JAMES, *sixteen*

NELL, *eighteen*
ANTHONY, *eighteen*

A
B

FRIEND ONE, *between fifteen and seventeen*
FRIEND TWO, *between fifteen and seventeen*

Note on Play

There are twenty-eight characters in this play. Some are female; some are male; some haven't been assigned to either gender. Please feel free to change the sex of characters where appropriate to suit availability. The characters can be played by individuals or by a company of actors who play several parts each. All characters are between the ages of eleven and twenty.

Setting

The entire play is set within one wardrobe. We travel through time visiting this wardrobe at specific moments throughout its history.

Scenes

Guidance for National Theatre Connections Participants 2014:

Only nine of the total twelve scenes can be performed. Participants are free to choose their preferred scenes. This rule can also be applied to subsequent productions of the play.

Acknowledgements

Sam wishes to thank all who helped develop, edit and support the writing of this play, including Anthony Banks, Rob Watt, Lucy Deere, Tom Lyons, Matthew Poxon, Alastair Muriel, Richard and Katherine Polson, Mel Kenyon and all at Nick Hern Books. Thanks also to the Tricycle Theatre's Young Company for their help to workshop the play during the early stages of development.

Prologue

In view is a huge and imposing wardrobe dating from the late-fifteenth century. The effect is handmade, of solid oak, with detailed carving and beautifully panelled double doors with ornamental holes, which allow in the light. It is an impressive presence.

The wardrobe rotates revealing to the audience its rear side. The back of the wardrobe has no wall, allowing the audience to see its contents. We are privy to anything that takes place within the confines of its walls. The inside of this wardrobe is our stage. The wardrobe is large enough to fit at least four people at any one time.

Scene One

The bedchamber of ELIZABETH OF YORK, *the Royal Court, London, 27th October 1485, afternoon.*

Tudor Court music or similar sounds of the time and place could be used to set the scene.

The Wars of the Roses have raged for thirty years between the houses of York and Lancaster (whose heraldic symbols were the white and red rose respectively) for the English throne.

Following the defeat and death of the Yorkist King, Richard III, at the Battle of Bosworth, the conquering hero, and Lancastrian heir, Henry Tudor, ascends to the throne as King Henry VII of England. Nieces of the defeated King Richard III, ELIZABETH *and her younger sister,* CECILY OF YORK, *reside at Court in anticipation of the coronation of their new King.*

The door of the wardrobe opens, CECILY *climbs inside. She closes the door behind her, pushes aside the hanging robes and sits. She scowls. After a moment, the door opens and* ELIZABETH *enters and closes the door behind her. Bright daylight filters through the ornamental holes, dappling them with light.*

ELIZABETH. There you are. Move aside.

ELIZABETH *sinks down beside* CECILY.

Well, 'tis official: a letter from the King was published in the Parliament house just this morn. Shall I read it to you? (*Holding the parchment up to candlelight and reciting.*) 'Henry, by the grace of God, King of England and France, Prince of Wales, and Lord of Ireland, ascertaineth you that Richard Duke of Gloucester, lately called King Richard, was slain at a place called Sandeford and there laid openly that every man might look upon him: God have mercy on his soul. And, moreover, the King, our Sovereign Lord, shall wed the lady Elizabeth of York to the pleasure of Almighty God, the wealth, prosperity and surety of this Realm of England.' (*With sarcasm.*) Oh, Cecily, how it puts to shame the greatest love poems!

CECILY *giggles*.

He has no intention to share power, thus his coronation will occur afore marriage. Can you believe your ears, Cecily? I've eaten partridges with a stronger royal lineage. Besides, he's so old.

CECILY. He's thirty.

ELIZABETH. Exactly, he's *ancient*. And he has such a long face. I do not care to look at my husband and think of my horse. Henry Tudor. He'll insist we name our firstborn son after him. What shall that make him? Henry... the Eighth. How tedious! No, I shan't have that. I'll start a new fashion: Barnaby the First.

CECILY. We cannot have King Barnaby.

ELIZABETH. Why not?

CECILY. It sounds absurd.

ELIZABETH. Humphrey.

CECILY. No.

ELIZABETH. Arthur, then.

CECILY. King Arthur?

ELIZABETH. In honour of the legendary King Arthur and his Knights of the Round Table. On this I shan't negotiate. I am the daughter of King Edward the Fourth; sister to King Edward the Fifth – if I weren't a woman, Cecily, no one would question my right to rule my country. But because I have a womb and breasts he'll not share his crown with me, only his bed. I've half a mind to deny him.

CECILY. He'd confine you to the Tower.

ELIZABETH. So be it.

CECILY. Oh, hush your ridiculous brabbling! You know not how lucky you are. One day they will write books about you, plays about you: Elizabeth of York, the White Princess, who married the Red King and thus ended the Wars of the Roses.

But what of her sister, Cecily? Who ever heard of her? I expect she died alone in a convent!

CECILY *attempts to exit the wardrobe.* ELIZABETH *stops her and produces a silver spoon.*

ELIZABETH. I have found a spoon. I think it is silver. Six points?

CECILY *snatches the spoon and gnaws at it with her teeth.*

Cecily!

Her gnawing reveals some other metal underneath: it is only silver-plated.

Oh. Three points? One point.

CECILY. Half a point.

ELIZABETH. Half a point! Fine. Have you done any better?

CECILY *digs in her pocket and retrieves a jewelled dagger.*

Wherever did you find that!

CECILY. The courtyard.

CECILY *unsheathes the dagger. She cuts the air with it. The light glints off the blade.*

ELIZABETH. Well. Ten points?

CECILY. Ten? These are rubies. One hundred. At least.

ELIZABETH. Very well then.

ELIZABETH *prises open a board in the base of the wardrobe and hunts underneath.*

Oh yes. He said something else. If I die, he intends to marry you.

CECILY *looks at the dagger in her hand and then at her sister's exposed back.* ELIZABETH *retrieves a box from the base of the wardrobe and opens it. She takes out a scorecard and a stick of charcoal. She writes.*

Half a point to me. One hundred points to you.

CECILY *looks between her sister's back and the dagger.*

(*Still with her back to her sister.*) He had Uncle Richard's body stripped naked and tied to the side of his horse. They paraded the horse in town. Richard killed Edward; Henry kills Richard; who will kill Henry? It is a game of death, Cecily, and we have no choice but to play it. They thought nothing of killing our brothers. We, too, must be prepared to do things of which we never thought ourselves capable.

Again, ELIZABETH *rummages in the base of the wardrobe.* CECILY *raises the dagger to plunge it into her sister's back. Suddenly* ELIZABETH *swings into view a short-handled axe. The girls face each other with their weapons.*

I do not know what I would do without you. You are my best friend. I will see that you are always provided for. You will marry a gentleman and have many babies. I promise you this: you will never die alone in a convent, not while I am alive and we are sisters.

ELIZABETH *uses the edge of her axe to slice her hand and spill some blood.*

And while the same blood courses our veins, I solemnly swear, here and now, that I will do everything in my power to see that you never come to any harm.

She offers her hand to her sister for shaking.

CECILY *slices her hand on the blade of the dagger, she cries out in pain.* ELIZABETH *quickly presses her bloodied hand to her sister's mouth to silence her and unintentionally smears blood all over her face.* CECILY *pulls* ELIZABETH*'s hand away.*

CECILY. Urgh!

CECILY *spits* ELIZABETH*'s blood from her mouth.*

ELIZABETH. Oh, frothy boggarts, I am sorry!

CECILY. Urgh, your blood!

ELIZABETH. Sorry.

CECILY. You just made me eat your blood! Urgh!

ELIZABETH. Well, I did not mean to. It was supposed to be a… symbolic moment.

CECILY *wipes her tongue on her dress.*

Sorry. We can still shake on it.

CECILY. If I have to eat yours, then you have to eat mine.

ELIZABETH. What?

CECILY. It is only fair.

ELIZABETH. Well, that is not really how you are supposed to do it.

CECILY *shoves her bloody hand over her sister's mouth and holds her nose.* ELIZABETH *has to open her mouth to breath and gets a mouthful of her sister's blood. She throws her hand off and coughs and spits.*

Urgh. Pleurghh!

The two girls stare at each other with bloody faces.

CECILY. You look like a witch, a child-eater!

ELIZABETH. *You* look like a child-eater!

They crack a smile and laugh. The laughter trails away. They look at one another with sadness.

I don't want to marry him.

CECILY. I don't want to marry him either.

They embrace tightly and urgently.

ELIZABETH. He says I'm to leave my belongings. He'll buy me new clothes and a wardrobe in which to hang them.

ELIZABETH *touches a hand to the wall of the wardrobe.*

It belonged to our brothers; then 'twas mine; now 'tis yours.

VOICE (*calling from off*). Elizabeth!

The girls break apart.

ELIZABETH. Oh, God's death!

CECILY (*grabbing the axe, dagger and spoon*). Go, go, I'll put them away. Go!

ELIZABETH *wipes her face.*

ELIZABETH. How do I look?

CECILY. Tired.

ELIZABETH. You are supposed to say, 'Like a queen.' And then we're supposed to have another 'symbolic moment'.

CECILY. How many 'symbolic moments' do you want to have, Elizabeth?

ELIZABETH (*scoffing*). Very well then.

ELIZABETH *kisses her sister and exits.*

CECILY *returns their stash of stolen goods to the secret compartment. She hesitates on the dagger, staring at it a moment, before burying the thought along with the dagger below.*

She exits the wardrobe.

Scene Two

The house of the Santamaria family, England, 12th May 1633, evening.

Christian hymns or similar sounds of the time and place could be used to set the scene.

Since the late-thirteenth century Jews have not been permitted legally to reside in England.

During the Spanish Inquisition, the Ben-Moshe family (of Jewish descent) converts to Christianity under duress. They adopt the name of the church in which they were baptised, the Santa Maria, before being expelled from Spain and fleeing to England. Here they maintain the Jewish traditions of their ancestors in secret while publically adhering to the Protestant faith.

Brothers BENJAMIN *and* DANIEL *sit opposite each other in the wardrobe practising Hebrew. A candle or lantern glows between them, filling the space with warm light. (Female performers could play the siblings as sisters:* RUTH, *the elder sister, and* ABIGAIL, *the younger. If so, references to 'brother' should be changed to 'sister', and changes need to be made to the gender of the words spoken in Hebrew. Plus, the question in the opening section of dialogue, 'Are you a woman?' should be swapped with 'Are you a man?')*

BENJAMIN. 'I.'

DANIEL. *Ani.*

BENJAMIN. 'I want.'

DANIEL. *Ani… rotsa.*

BENJAMIN. Are you a woman?

DANIEL. No.

BENJAMIN. Then you do not say, '*Ani Rotsa,*' but '*Ani Rotse*'. Say it.

DANIEL. *Ani Rotse.*

BENJAMIN. Good. What is 'fish'?

DANIEL. *Dag*.

BENJAMIN. So all together: 'I want one fish.'

DANIEL. *Ani rotse dag a^at*.

BENJAMIN. No, 'fish' is masculine. So the 'one' has to reflect
the masculinity of the fish, and so you must say '*e^ad*' not
'*a^at*,' yes? Again.

DANIEL. *Ani rotse dag e^ad*.

BENJAMIN. Good, very good. 'I want one fish and three cakes.'

   DANIEL *groans*.

   Daniel.

DANIEL. *Ani rotse dag e^ad ve'shalosh ugat*.

BENJAMIN. I want one fish, three cakes and a bracelet.

DANIEL. Do we have to?

BENJAMIN. Yes.

DANIEL. It seems such a waste of time.

   Beat.

BENJAMIN. Forgive me, brother. You are right: your time
could be so much better spent adventuring for treasures in
your nostrils and depositing them on the rims of cups.

DANIEL. I don't do that. Any more. Besides, today I did in fact
unearth a treasure.

BENJAMIN. From your nose?

DANIEL. From the market – such a thing as you have never
seen!

   DANIEL *reaches into his pocket;* BENJAMIN *stops him*.

BENJAMIN. No.

DANIEL. But wait till you see it!

BENJAMIN. I said no. We came in here to study.

DANIEL. But I'm never going to ask anybody for one fish, three cakes and a bracelet in Hebrew: this is 1633 and we live in England! So what is the point?

BENJAMIN. 'Tis the language of our ancestors.

DANIEL. Our ancestors are dead.

Beat.

BENJAMIN. What has taken hold of you?

DANIEL. Nothing.

BENJAMIN. What happened?

DANIEL. Nothing happened. I'm just sick of the hypocrisy. We go to church on Sunday and beg forgiveness for our sins from Jesus Christ, then run home, hide in our wardrobe, and whisper in a forbidden language. 'Tis no wonder they call us filthy, lying, *merranos*!

DANIEL *attempts to exit;* BENJAMIN *stops him.*

BENJAMIN. Where did you hear that?

DANIEL. Why do you not teach me French?

BENJAMIN. Who said that to you?

DANIEL. Or Dutch, or something actually useful? Do you not want to travel and see the world? Today I saw things that took my breath away.

DANIEL *reaches into his pocket.*

BENJAMIN. Who called you a *merrano*? Daniel, 'tis very important that you –

DANIEL *pulls from his pocket a banana and holds it aloft.* BENJAMIN *stops short and stares. Neither boy has ever seen one in their life before today.*

What is that?

DANIEL. Is it not magnificent!

BENJAMIN *takes the banana from* DANIEL.

BENJAMIN. How strange... (*Sniffing the banana.*) Most peculiar... Is it a lemon?

DANIEL. No. No, it is absolutely not a lemon. But 'tis a fruit.

BENJAMIN. Is it poisonous?

DANIEL. No, I saw a man eat three in a row and walk away unscathed.

BENJAMIN *sniffs the banana again.*

'Tis from Bermuda!

BENJAMIN. Bermuda...?

DANIEL *nods.*

Does it have a name?

DANIEL. Indeed. They call it the – (*Mispronouncing.*) banana.

BENJAMIN. The – (*Repeating the mispronunciation.*) banana?

DANIEL. Yes. Apparently it is sweet, and sticky.

BENJAMIN (*mispronouncing*). Banana...

BENJAMIN *sticks out his tongue and tentatively licks the banana skin. He grimaces.*

Urgh.

DANIEL. No, you grout-head, we have to peel it first.

BENJAMIN *searches the banana for an obvious way to peel it; it perplexes him.*

BENJAMIN. Well... how do I get in?

BENJAMIN *attempts to snap the stalk (as we would normally do).*

DANIEL. No, that is the handle.

BENJAMIN. The handle?

DANIEL. Of course. Hold it by the handle.

BENJAMIN *holds the banana by the stalk.*

Now, I only saw him do this once...

DANIEL *proceeds to peel the banana as a monkey would by pinching the dry, brown, blossom end of the banana between the forefinger and thumb of each hand and peeling the two sides apart to reveal the fruit inside. They both marvel at it.*

Go on.

BENJAMIN *takes a bite of the banana. He chews it slowly. DANIEL takes a bite and chews slowly as well. After a moment they both nod in approval.*

It is sweet.

BENJAMIN. And soft.

DANIEL. Mushy.

BENJAMIN. Sticky.

DANIEL. It is like sticky mashed potatoes.

BENJAMIN. With honey.

DANIEL. Yes.

BENJAMIN. Most...

DANIEL. Satisfying. (*Reaching into his pocket and retrieving a second banana.*) I have another.

BENJAMIN. If you were at the market, then you were not at school.

DANIEL. Shall I open it or would you like to try?

BENJAMIN. Why were you not at school? Daniel?

DANIEL *reaches into his pocket again, and instead of another banana he retrieves a quarto, a printed pamphlet, and tosses it toward* BENJAMIN. BENJAMIN *reads the front cover aloud.*

The Famous Tragedy of the Rich Jew of Malta by Christopher Marlowe.

DANIEL. There is to be a revival by the Queen Henrietta's Men at the Cockpit Theatre in London. I am going to see it with my class. Oliver Goodwyn said, in front of everybody, that I was surely looking forward to wallowing in the mud of my Jewish ancestry like the *merrano* pig I am. (*Beat.*) I do not see why I should be despised because of who my great-great-grandparents were. I never met them. I can't even speak their boil-brained language!

Pause.

BENJAMIN. I know you wish to be like everybody else. But rather than thinking of yourself as different, why not think of yourself as having a secret instead?

Beat.

DANIEL. A secret? (*Scoffing.*) I'm not a child: I'm thirteen.

BENJAMIN. I am eighteen and I think of it as a secret; a secret we share. The same secret our mother and father share. And their mother and father before them. And this… (*Gesturing to the confines of the wardrobe.*) this is a place for secrets.

DANIEL. This is a wardrobe.

BENJAMIN. That's what a wardrobe is for – to guard your secrets. Warden, warder, wardrobe. And it is nearly one hundred and fifty years old. So imagine what secrets it has kept guard over in all that time. Father says it belonged to the aunt of King Henry the Eighth. Cecily something.

DANIEL. Really…

BENJAMIN. But she fell out of favour and the King banished her to live in a nunnery, and sold all her belongings! When our grandfather fled Spain and came to this country he bought these pieces of English tradition. He wrapped them around himself like a disguise.

DANIEL. Like a masked hero…

BENJAMIN. Yes, exactly. But on the inside, in here, we take off the mask and be ourselves. Our ancestors may be dead, but when we admit to who we truly are we keep their spirit alive.

Beat.

DANIEL. What if I do not want a secret? I did not ask for it.

BENJAMIN. Nobody ever asks for a secret. A secret asks for you.

DANIEL. How long do I have to keep it?

BENJAMIN. Not long. There will be synagogue in London in our lifetime.

DANIEL. Do you really think so?

BENJAMIN. And when we go there, do you want to be the only one who cannot ask for a one fish, three cakes and a banana in Hebrew? Is banana masculine or feminine? What do you think?

They both look at the second, unpeeled banana.

TOGETHER. Masculine.

BENJAMIN. So then: one fish, three cakes and a banana.

DANIEL. *Ani rotse dag e^ad ve'uga shalosha ve'banana.*

The brothers smile at one another.

Scene Three

*A master bedroom of the Ainsley family home, Bolton, England,
28th May 1644, afternoon.*

*Gunfire and explosions or similar sounds of the time and place
could be used to set the scene.*

*The first English Civil War between the Parliamentarians and
the Royalists enters its third year. The strongly Parliamentarian
town of Bolton, near Manchester, is stormed and captured by
the Royalists under Prince Rupert of the Rhine. Unlike a formal
siege, usually preceded by a parlay and ended by a negotiated
surrender, the suddenness of the attack leaves the town without
the protection of any laws or contemporary conventions of
warfare, and the Royalist soldiers are allowed to plunder the
town and take whatever and whomever they want as reward.*

*Two of the Ainsley children, MATILDA and HENRY, seek
shelter in the wardrobe. Dull afternoon light shines though the
ornamental holes, casting them in shadow. They shake with fear
and hold each other close. Suddenly the door handle turns.
MATILDA screams. HENRY struggles to jam the door handle
shut but he's not strong enough – the door opens. TOBIAS, the
third of the Ainsley children, enters. He is wet from the rain.
HENRY stifles MATILDA's scream by clamping a hand over
her mouth. Sounds of screaming and gunfire can be heard
beyond the wardrobe through the window of the bedroom out
onto the street.*

HENRY. Toby! Matilda, it's only Toby!

   HENRY *pulls* TOBIAS *into the wardrobe.*

MATILDA (*embracing* TOBIAS). Oh, Toby, thank Heaven –
   you're alive!

TOBIAS. Matilda, Henry – are you hurt?

MATILDA. No, we're well. (*Noticing blood on his clothes.*)
   You're bleeding.

TOBIAS. 'Tis not mine.

   MATILDA *stares in horror at the blood.*

MATILDA. Where is Mother?

TOBIAS *doesn't answer.*

No... oh no...

HENRY *makes to exit the wardrobe.*

TOBIAS. No, Henry!

TOBIAS *grabs his brother and bars his exit from the wardrobe.*

Henry, pray listen to me: you cannot go out there – it's bedlam! They're shooting people in the streets, there's blood and rain running in the gutters, you can hardly breathe for musket smoke.

HENRY. But I must find her.

TOBIA (*holding him back*). I saw a boy insult a soldier and the soldier smashed his head with a rifle butt.

MATILDA. Then, I'll go.

TOBIAS (*barring MATILDA's exit*). Women are lying in the streets, dresses torn from their bodies. They are Royalist pigs and they'll show you no mercy – you cannot go outside. We have no choice but to hide in here.

MATILDA. But Mother...

TOBIAS. 'Tis too late.

MATILDA *weeps.*

All will be well. I promise you. How often have we played in here? No harm could come to us in here.

The door of the wardrobe rattles. HENRY and TOBIAS pull on the handle to keep the door shut. A serving girl, CARYL, can be heard calling through the door.

CARYL (*calling from off*). 'Tis Caryl. Let me in!

MATILDA. Toby, 'tis Caryl, she works in the kitchen.

CARYL (*calling from off*). Please, Sir Tobias! Mistress Matilda, let me in!

MATILDA. Toby, let her inside.

TOBIAS. There's no room. (*Calling through the door.*) You'll have to find somewhere else.

CARYL. Please, they're coming. They're coming!

HENRY. Let her in, Toby.

MATILDA. Toby, let her in!

TOBIAS *opens the door and pulls* CARYL *into the wardrobe. He slams the door shut behind her. She has blood on her face and in her hair.*

CARYL (*shaking with fear*). They pulled Elsie into the street by her hair. Her hand got trapped in the door.

TOBIAS. Shush.

CARYL. 'Tis still there on the mat.

TOBIAS. Be quiet!

CARYL *falls silent. The four of them organise themselves within the wardrobe. They are pressed up against the walls; possibly one is pushed into a sitting position while the others stand. Perhaps they pile on top of each other. There is hardly any room to move at all.*

CARYL. I can't, ouch –

MATILDA. Henry, you're squashing me!

CARYL. Ow!

TOBIAS. Quiet! Nobody make a sound!

An unspecified noise is heard beyond the wardrobe. They freeze in terror.

MATILDA. What was that?

TOBIAS *puts his fingers to his sister's lips.* CARYL'*s breathing becomes laboured. Another unspecified sound is heard beyond the wardrobe.*

CARYL. I… please, can you –

ALL. Shhh!

CARYL. I'm sorry, I can't… I can't breathe… in small spaces, please…

TOBIAS. Be quiet, Caryl.

CARYL. I'm sorry, I can't –

MATILDA. Caryl, there is somebody outside.

CARYL. No, you have to let me out. Help.

TOBAIS. Caryl, be quiet.

CARYL (*with rising hysteria*). Help. Help me.

> TOBIAS *clamps a hand over* CARYL's *mouth.* CARYL *fights to pull it off.*

MATILDA. Please, Caryl.

HENRY. Shh, Caryl.

MATILDA. If they find us, they'll kill us.

> CARYL *begins to struggle.* TOBIAS *applies increasing force to restrain her.*

CARYL (*pulling his hand off*). Let me out, help! Help me!

> *The others attempt to restrain her. They push and pull her down onto the floor of the wardrobe; they pull a dress off a hanger and smother her mouth.* CARYL *kicks and flails, but they apply pressure until the kicking and flailing subsides.* CARYL *suffocates and dies. Suddenly footsteps can be heard just beyond the wardrobe. They freeze. The door handle of the wardrobe turns. An explosion is heard beyond the house in the street. The door handle is released and the footsteps recede and disappear.*

> *They look at* CARYL *who lies limp in their arms.*

HENRY (*attempting to leave*). I think I shall be sick.

TOBIAS (*holding* HENRY *back*). No, you can't go out there.

HENRY. They've gone.

TOBIAS. How can you know? They might come back. We must stay in here.

HENRY. I can't, not with…

TOBIAS. You must.

HENRY. She's dead. We killed her.

MATILDA (*gently rocking* CARYL). There, there, Caryl…

HENRY. We killed her.

TOBIAS. Listen very carefully: we came into the bedroom and we found her like this. A Royalist pig soldier had smothered her to death because she served a Parliamentarian family. We brought her into the wardrobe with us so that her body might not be defiled. She will never be a prisoner of Prince Rupert of the Rhine because now she is free.

MATILDA. There now, Caryl…

HENRY. How long shall we stay in here?

TOBIAS. All night if we must.

> HENRY *leans against the wall, exhausted;* TOBIAS *stands guard;* MATILDA *gently rocks* CARYL *in her arms.*

MATILDA. Hush now, Caryl… all will be well…

Scene Four

A bedroom of the Barwicke family home London, England, 18th September 1665, morning.

Baroque music or similar sounds of the time and place could be used to set the scene.

The Great Plague of London is at its height. The Barwicke family have evacuated to Oxfordshire, leaving the house under the rule of the servants. Ladies' maids ANNE, MARY *and* SARAH *abscond from their duties to gossip in the wardrobe. Bright morning light shines through the ornamental holes.*

SARAH. I find it most amusing: (*Referring to the wardrobe.*) the mistress spends a royal fortune on the furniture only to flee to the country leaving it to stand empty.

MARY. I find it most convenient: since they left, there's been nothing to do.

ANNE. I find it most inconvenient: the less there is to do, the more Red-faced Ramsey hounds us.

SARAH. Would he ever think to look in here?

ANNE. Imagine if he did – three girls in one cupboard!

The girls laugh and imitate Red-faced Ramsay.

I'm so bored. I want to go for a walk, I want to eat hot rolls fresh from the bakery – I want to go to the theatre!

The others groan; they've heard this a thousand times before.

SARAH (*imitating* ANNE). The King's Company has followed King Charles to Oxford!

MARY (*imitating* ANNE). They perform privately for him, don't you know!

SARAH (*imitating* ANNE). I am jealous beyond all measure!

ANNE. Mock me all you want, but as soon as the Company returns I shall go straight to the Theatre Manager, Thomas Killigrew, and dazzle him with my audition piece.

SARAH *and* MARY (*imitating* ANNE). 'Audition piece.'

SARAH. Yes, we know.

MARY. Why do you so desire to be an actress?

SARAH. Oh, please don't encourage her.

ANNE. I remember as though it were yesterday, the first actress to ever grace the stage: Margaret Hughes playing Desdemona. Oh, it caused such a stir! She was magnificent. I knew then there was nothing else I'd rather do.

SARAH. My father says that all actresses are... *ladies of the night*.

ANNE. Well, performances are early evening actually, plus a Saturday matinee.

MARY. She means 'prostitute'.

ANNE. Prostitute! Your father said that all actresses are prostitutes?

SARAH. Well, not exactly.

ANNE. What exactly did he say?

SARAH. Pox-ridden, festering whores. He said they're to be shunned like the pla–

SARAH *stops short of uttering the word 'plague.' There follows a short pause.*

ANNE. Mark you, I am not the sort of girl to be selling anything other than my talent. Await the day, for it shall come, when all shall know my name.

ANNE *takes a small instrument out of her pocket and carves her initials into the wall of the wardrobe.*

They will say it all over town. You will hear my name called from the taverns to the turrets of the tower.

MARY (*reading the inscription*). A–R.

ANNE. Anne Ransford! This wardrobe will be worth a fortune for the simple fact of my having trodden its boards. (*Beat.*)

I just wish they would hurry home so I can perform my audition piece.

MARY. Show us then.

SARAH. Oh, Lord above…

MARY. Ignore her. Go on.

SARAH. If you must.

ANNE *stands and recites a speech from Shakespeare (a speech from* Macbeth *is used as an example, but this could be substituted for any other).*

ANNE.
The raven himself is hoarse,
That croaks the fatal entrance of Duncan
Under my battlements. Come, you spirits
That tend on mortal thoughts, unsex me here,
And fill me from the crown to the toe top-full
Of direst cruelty! Make thick –

SARAH *coughs.*

SARAH (*clearing her throat*). Sorry, carry on.

ANNE.
                    Make thick my blood;
Stop up the access and passage to remorse,
That no compunctious visitings of nature
Shake my fell purpose, nor keep peace between –

SARAH *coughs a second time. Again,* ANNE *and* MARY *look at* SARAH *with rising alarm.*

SARAH. It's very good. Who wrote it? Play on.

ANNE.
Come. Come to my woman's breasts.
And take my milk for gall, you murdering ministers,
Wherever in your sightless substances
You wait on nature's mischief! Come thick night
And pall thee in the dunnest smoke of hell – !

SARAH *coughs; when she takes her hand away from her mouth there is blood on her fingers.*

SARAH. It's not... it's just a cough.

Suddenly the others pounce on her; they pull up her dress to look for signs of plague (buboes/swollen lymph glands) on her thighs. SARAH fights them.

It is just a cough. Coughing is not even a symptom! Stop it!

The girls search her thighs but find no evidence of plague.

See? There's nothing.

The girls feel in her armpits; they find nothing.

I don't have it. I do not have the plague.

MARY *and* ANNE *sigh with relief; they lean back and catch their breath.*

MARY. Sorry, Sarah.

ANNE. Yes, sorry.

SARAH. What would you have done? Thrown me out onto the street? I have nowhere else to go.

MARY. Nor I.

ANNE. Nor I.

SARAH. Go on, then. Finish your audition speech. It was quite good.

ANNE (*wiping perspiration from her forehead and reciting once more*).
Come thick night
And pall thee in the dunnest smoke of hell,
That my keen knife...
Not see the wound it makes
Nor heaven peep... peep through the blanket of the dark
To cry, H– Hold!

ANNE *cries out in agony, she sinks to the ground.*

MARY. Bravo!

SARAH. Very realistic.

MARY. Anne?

SARAH *applauds*.

Sarah, stop. I think she is serious. Anne?

SARAH. Anne?

MARY. Anne, what is it? Where does it hurt?

MARY *and* SARAH *pounce on her. They pull up her dress to reveal buboes across her thighs. They recoil in fear.* ANNE *pulls down her dress in shame.*

(*Making to leave.*) We need to call a doctor.

ANNE. There are no doctors left. Even so, who would care about me? Who would hurry to the bedside of a serving girl? (*Reaching out a hand.*) Please do not leave me.

MARY. We can't touch you. You know that. We can't even stand beside you.

ANNE *withdraws her hand and lies down to weep.*

(*Making to leave.*) Sarah? Come.

SARAH. Wait.

SARAH *pulls a robe off a hanger and dresses in it backwards as though it were a doctor's gown; she finds a pair of silk gloves hanging on the rail and pulls them on.*

(*To* MARY.) Help me.

MARY *fastens the robe at her back. She tends to* ANNE.

Await the day, for it shall come when all shall know thy name. They'll say it all over town. We'll hear thy name called from the taverns to the turrets of the tower, Anne Ransford.

MARY *ties a scarf around* SARAH's *mouth to act as a facemask.* MARY *pulls on a pair of gloves. The two girls lift* ANNE *off the floor and help her to exit the wardrobe.*

Scene Five

Any time between 1665 and 1770, night.

The wardrobe is no longer in England and has instead been sold to a family abroad.

(This scene is to be translated into whichever language is relevant or interesting to the players.)

Music or sounds relevant to the time and place could be used to set the scene.

ONE *teaches* TWO *how to defend against attack. They work by the light of a lantern of a style native to the time and place.* ONE *has* TWO *in a chokehold.*

ONE. What do you do? What do you do?

> TWO *places her/his hands on* ONE's *arms and attempts to remove them. (S)he is unsuccessful.*

I am stronger than you. You have to get out of my grip. What do you do?

TWO *doesn't respond*

Lift your right arm. Lift your right arm.

TWO *reluctantly lifts her/his right arm.*

Swing it over my head and turn away from me. Do it.

TWO *reluctantly swings her/his right arm in an anticlockwise motion over* ONE's *head and turns around so that (s)he is facing away from* ONE.

See, I've lost my hold on your neck. Yes? Now bend your left arm and raise your elbow. Aim for my head. (*Demonstrating.*) Bend your elbow like this thrust it into the side of his head. One clean motion. (*Demonstrates the whole manoeuvre: swinging over the head with the right arm and punching with the left elbow.*) See? Yes? Your turn. Come on. Quickly.

TWO *attempts the manoeuvre.*

Over with the right; up with the left. Faster.

TWO *attempts to do the manoeuvre more quickly.*

Yes, good, run.

ONE *pushes* TWO *away.*

But he will come after you. (*Catching* TWO*'s wrists from behind.*) He will try to stop you.

ONE *now holds* TWO *securely by the wrists from behind.*

What do you do?

TWO *half-heartedly wriggles her/his wrists to try and get free.*

Pull your hands forward as though you were lifting a weight.

ONE *demonstrates the manoeuvre: s(he) lifts her hands as thought (s)he were lifting weights.*

He will lose his grip and then, as before, you turn to face him and punch with your elbow. Try it.

TWO *reluctantly attempts the manoeuvre.*

Use your weight. Faster. Yes. But if he comes after you again...

ONE *presses* TWO *up against the wall of the wardrobe.*

What do you do?

TWO *struggles to break free of* ONE*'s grip.*

No, that's what he wants. He wants to exhaust you. He will keep going until there is no fight left in you. So what do you do?

TWO (*pushing* ONE *away in frustration*). I don't know.

Beat.

ONE. If a small bird flies into the room and I catch her in my hands what will she do? She will flap her wings and struggle, and I will tighten my grip around her until she is spent. But if instead she lies still and says, 'Please don't hurt me. Do what you want with me. I won't struggle,' she convinces me she has nothing left, I open my hands and she takes off and flies away.

ONE *pushes* TWO *up against the wall again.*

If he comes after you again, what do you do?

TWO *struggles against* ONE.

TWO. No, stop it. I don't want to do this any more. Get off me.

ONE. Don't fight, that's what he wants.

TWO (*fighting*). I said get off. Get off me!

TWO *struggles, but* ONE *is too strong for her/him; s(he) remains pinned against the wall. Eventually (s)he surrenders.*

Please don't hurt me. Do what you want with me. I won't struggle.

ONE *relaxes his/her grip on* TWO. *Immediately* TWO *completes the self-defence manoeuvre: (s)he swings an arm over* ONE'*s head, turns away and raises her/his elbow to affect a blow to the head. It is a proficient move.* ONE *is taken by surprise.*

ONE. Good. Good. Again.

Scene Six

A bedroom of Kenwood House, Hampstead, London, 5th May 1780, afternoon.

Music by Mozart or similar sounds of the time and place could be used to set the scene.

DIDO ELIZABETH BELLE *is the illegitimate daughter of Sir John Lindsay, a British Navy captain, and an enslaved woman whom Sir John encountered while his ship was in the Caribbean.* DIDO *is mixed race. She resides in the house of her childless great-uncle, William Murray, Lord Mansfield. A decade earlier, Lord Mansfield, a leading judge, passed a famous judgment in court freeing a slave from imprisonment by his master on the basis that slavery was unsupported by law in England and Wales (although this did not end slave trafficking in Britain altogether).*

The door to the wardrobe opens, and DIDO *quietly enters. She pushes aside the dresses hanging on the rail and clears a space for herself. The afternoon sun filters through the ornamental holes, piercing her with shards of light. She kneels on the floor and clasps her hands in prayer. She hesitates, strains to listen, and when satisfied that nobody can hear her, begins to pray.*

DIDO. Dear God, my heavenly father, thank you for today. Thank you for the good weather we enjoyed and for the birds outside my window. Thank you most especially for the fat pigeon that comes to rest in the old oak. I have named him Charlie. Fat Charlie. Thank you for coffee – powerful, rich coffee. I'm grateful for the strong flavour that cuts through my sluggish morning mouth. I'm grateful for the two hours' work I did this morning. I'm grateful for the pages I edited, and the progress I helped Uncle William to make with his accounts. I'm grateful that you can't get lead poisoning from stabbing yourself with a pencil. Thank you for that lovely moment just now when I mouthed to Uncle William, 'I love you,' and he mouthed in return, 'I love you too, my dear.' I am so grateful to have the love of this family. What else...? Oh yes, I'm so grateful that I am no longer scared of bees. And thank you for this beautiful wardrobe, which my uncle gave to me so I might hang my beautiful clothes in here. Thank you for the smell of the wood, and the reassuring feel of the panels under my knees holding me up. Thank you for a place I can come to when I need to be alone. Thank you also for the fact I could talk to Elizabeth for an hour about her upcoming trip to the Derby race and I didn't feel hopelessly dissatisfied that I will not attend. I am learning that the secret to happiness is not how successful you are, or what people say about you, or how you look, or whether your parents were married, but whether or not you can be thankful for what you have. And so, right now, in this moment, I am grateful to my uncle and his wife for all they have done for me and rescued me from. Today I am so grateful that I am not enslaved upon a ship, as my mother was. I am so grateful to my uncle that he struck down slavery in court. And because of him I live without fear of torture and oppression. I don't know why I've been dealt such a fortunate hand, but to whomever is responsible for my lucky, lucky fate I am truly, truly thankful. Even though my illegitimacy and the colour of my skin mean that I am not eligible to eat with the family at the table, or join their guests for dinner, or attend the Derby with Elizabeth, I am so thankful that the women do invite me to join them for coffee when supper is done. I am so grateful they afford me that kindness; they show me such unwavering generosity.

Suddenly she pulls a dress violently off a hanger and throws it down; she smacks the wall of the wardrobe in distress. She cradles her injured hand. She catches her breath. She clasps her hands in prayer once again.

Forgive me, Father, forgive my ungratefulness. Forgive my indulgence, my impatience, my selfishness. (*Short pause.*) I'm grateful to the concept of gratefulness for giving me a way to encourage happy thoughts and feelings. Thank you for giving me a way out of the dark and into the light.

DIDO *kneels in silence for a moment. She kisses her hands and raises them to the heavens. She stands and smooths her dress. She stares into space for a moment, all enthusiasm lost, before bracing herself and exiting the wardrobe.*

Scene Seven

A child's bedroom of the Hughes family house, Liverpool, England, 2nd August 1805, morning.

Music by Beethoven or similar sounds of the time and place could be used to set the scene.

Britain has been a leader in the Atlantic slave trade for the past two centuries. While most of the slaves concerned are transported from Africa to the Americas, many arrive in England to work as household servants; some are paid while others are considered property. William Wilberforce's Slave Trade Act will not abolish the slave trade in the British Empire for another two years. Slavery itself will not be abolished in the British Empire for another twenty-eight years.

The door of the wardrobe opens and WILLIAM *enters.* WILLIAM *is an unpaid domestic servant to the Hughes family, brought to England from Africa as a slave at the age of three. He carries a freshly laundered coat belonging to his master's son,* JAFFREY. WILLIAM *hangs the coat on the rail and smoothes the cloth. Suddenly he climbs into the wardrobe and closes the door behind him. He takes the coat off the hanger and dresses in it. He runs his hands over the fine embroidery. Suddenly the door to the wardrobe opens and* JAFFREY *stands at the entrance staring at* WILLIAM; *it is clear* JAFFREY *has been crying. Morning light filters through the ornamental holes. (Female players could perform this scene by simply changing the names.)*

JAFFREY. William!

WILLIAM (*bowing his head in deference*). Master Jaffrey.

JAFFREY. Why are you wearing my coat?

WILLIAM. Forgive me.

JAFFREY. Take it off.

WILLIAM (*removing the coat*). Forgive me.

JAFFREY. Take it off at once.

WILLIAM (*returning the coat to its hanger*). I only meant to check the fit. I was hoping the process of steam-cleaning had not shrunk it.

JAFFREY. Wash it again. Return it to be washed again.

WILLIAM. Of course, Master Jaffrey.

JAFFREY. Out. Get. Out.

WILLIAM *bows to* JAFFREY *and exits;* JAFFREY *enters in his place and vents his frustrations on the clothes by shoving them aggressively aside and sinking onto the floor in a sulk. There is a knock on the door of the wardrobe; it startles* JAFFREY.

Yes?

WILLIAM. Master Jaffrey, it is I, William.

JAFFREY. Go away, William.

WILLIAM. Please may I –

JAFFREY (*opening the door of the wardrobe*). William, I said go away.

WILLIAM *climbs back inside the wardrobe, to* JAFFREY*'s surprise.*

WILLIAM. I am afraid I cannot do that, Master Jaffrey.

WILLIAM *closes the wardrobe door behind him, confining them both inside.*

JAFFREY. What are you doing?

WILLIAM. You see, if I return your coat to Miss Emily to clean, I shall have to explain why. And while I find it easy enough to lie to you, I should not like to lie to her.

JAFFREY. How dare you!

WILLIAM. For she will be forced to report the misdemeanour to my master, your father, and I cannot have him know, so we shall have to come to some agreement, as gentleman.

JAFFRREY. How can you call yourself a gentleman?

WILLIAM. You will not mention that I took the liberty of wearing your coat and you will not ask me to make mention of it either. And, in return, I will not mention what I saw pass between you and Master Arthur Scott, the night before last, in the passage leading from the library.

JAFFREY *stares at* WILLIAM *in horror. Suddenly he lunges at him and they struggle.* WILLIAM, *much the stronger, pins* JAFFREY *against the wall.*

JAFFREY. Let me go. Let me go at once!

WILLIAM. Do we have an agreement?

JAFFREY *wriggles free of* WILLIAM*'s grip and darts for the door.*

Do not doubt me, Master Jaffrey, I shall tell of what I saw!

JAFFREY (*stopping by the door*). If you dare, I shall see you hang for it, do you understand me? It would be so easy for me.

JAFFREY *pulls the coat off the rack and scrunches it into a ball.*

Father, my coat is missing... I last gave it to William to press... Father, do you think he might have stolen it? I remember I saw him admiring it the other day. He was touching it all over with his dirty fingers. We would watch you jerk and swing on the end of a rope within a week.

WILLIAM. The master would not believe me a thief.

JAFFREY. Oh, William... Poor deluded William... Do you really believe he would accept your word over mine? My father will never see you as a son. You are at best, a pet, at worst, nothing more than this wardrobe: to be bought and sold, one family to another.

WILLIAM. You need not see me as your rival; I do not seek his love.

JAFFREY. His love! William, you embarrass yourself. You'd do well to remember your station.

JAFFREY *turns to leave*.

WILLIAM. I have a friend who serves Arthur Scott's father.

JAFFREY *pauses by the door.*

My friend tells me he is a very cruel man, and that he is known to beat Arthur until his skin breaks. While I jerk and swing from a rope, you can be sure your good friend Arthur's bones will twist and break against his father's stick.

JAFFREY (*with sudden rage and alarm*). If any harm comes to Arthur, I swear will, I swear to God I will –

WILLIAM. What? What will you do? I will already have been hanged. Master Jaffrey, there is no need for any one to hang, or for any bones to break, or for any masters to be told secrets and lies. I will never mention to a living soul what I saw, if you agree to do the same.

JAFFREY *stares at him in anger.*

You've never liked me; I know it. I've never liked you. There's no shame in that; we cannot all like each other. Your father has promised to endow me with my freedom upon his death. On that day, I swear to it, you shall never see me again. You shan't have to wait long: his health worsens by the day.

JAFFREY. As does his temper.

Beat.

WILLIAM. So, then. Are we agreed?

WILLIAM *extends his hand to* JAFFREY *to shake on the deal.* JAFFREY *stares at his hand.*

There is a first time for everything.

JAFFREY *shakes* WILLIAM*'s hand*

It's settled then. Good day to you, Master Jaffrey.

WILLIAM *makes to exit.*

JAFFREY. William?

WILLIAM. Yes, Master Jaffrey.

JAFFREY (*handing* WILLIAM *the crumpled coat*). This needs pressing.

JAFFREY *exits the wardrobe.* WILLIAM *follows shortly after.*

Scene Eight

A child's bedroom of the Hughes family house, Liverpool, England, 9th July 1827.

During the years of the Industrial Revolution, as manufacture in Britain transitions from hand-production methods to machines, children as young as four are employed in factories with dangerous and often fatal working conditions. By the early-nineteenth century, England has more than one million child-workers who make up fifteen per cent of the labour force.

The doors to the wardrobe open and ROBERT *drags* MARTIN *inside, slamming the door shut.* MARTIN *carries a lit ship's lantern, which he uses to light the chimney for cleaning. (Female performers could play this scene by changing the names.)*

MARTIN. Get off me!

ROBERT. Get in there.

MARTIN. I weren't going to –

ROBERT. Keep yer voice down.

MARTIN (*more quietly*). I weren't going to take it. I were just lookin' at it.

ROBERT. You were just lookin' at it?

MARTIN. It were really shiny.

ROBERT. It were really shiny. Ain't nobody taught you how to lie better 'an that?

MARTIN. I ain't lying. I just, I just wanted to touch one of 'em. What's a person need that many teaspoons for anyhow? All lined up on display like that.

ROBERT. For eating jelly. That's right, they all congregate en masse and eat jelly.

MARTIN (*scratching*). What's 'en masse'.

ROBERT. It's French. For all together.

MARTIN (*scratching*). I ain't never spoke no French before.

ROBERT. Well, consider yourself... educated. Now, your
    master'll come lookin' for yer any minute, so you best get...
    You haven't got fleas, have yer?

MARTIN (*showing him the bites*). I got bites the size of pennies
    all the way up me leg. Look. You ain't seen nothing like it?

ROBERT (*looking*). Call 'em bites? I'll show you a bite.
    (*Lifting his trouser leg.*) Rat bite. Afore I worked in the main
    house I worked up the mill. Slept thirteen boys to one room.
    Bottom bunk weren't so much a bunk as the floor. Floor's
    crawling with 'em at night.

MARTIN. How do I know that ain't just a scar?

ROBERT. Cos I'm telling you it's a bite. You want a scar, I'll
    show you a scar. (*Pulling open his shirt collar to reveal
    scars around his neck.*) One morning I was late for work and
    the master made me wear weights round me neck and walk
    the length of the mill up and down. Each time I fell he added
    more weight.

MARTIN (*pulling up his shirt to reveal welts on his back*).
    Once I was late for work and the master beat me with his
    leather belt strap. See? That's where he caught me with the
    buckle.

ROBERT. That ain't worth a fart in a whirlwind. Look at this.
    (*Shows* MARTIN *patches of bald scalp.*) One night they left
    the doors unlocked. I made it as far as a field of pigs. I
    gorged on pig-feed. The master caught me, held me head on
    a bench and cut me hair off at the scalp with a meat cleaver;
    he took great chunks of skin. The hair ain't never grown
    back. And yer know what I says to him? I said, 'May the
    fleas of a thousand stray cats find your crotch, and may your
    arms be too short to scratch!' For a week he dragged me
    naked from my bed and made me join the assembly line
    holding me clothes.

    MARTIN *rolls up the sleeve of his shirt to reveal
    suppurating skin wounds on his elbows.* ROBERT *reels back
    in disgust.*

MARTIN. Comes from pressing your arms against the sides of the chimney, that way I can hold my body suspended, knees and elbows pressed against the walls, it peels the skin and the soot gets in, all different kinds of soot and that causes the festerin' – (*Rolling shirt higher.*) Look, takes weeks, sometimes months to heal.

ROBERT. I lost two teeth when I passed out on the stone floor from tiredness. We hardly got a wink of sleep, starting at five in the morning.

MARTIN. I start at four.

ROBERT. Six days a week, one meal a day.

MARTIN. Once I were so hungry I ate acorns.

ROBERT. Once I were so hungry I ate a turnip frozen out of the ground.

MARTIN. Once I were so hungry I ate cabbage.

ROBERT. What's wrong with cabbage?

MARTIN. I hate cabbage.

ROBERT. Once I were so hungry I was feeling faint while cleaning the loom that I didn't hear the man shouting for me to crawl out. He let go the brake and the carriage swung back into place and crushed me arm. I managed to pull it free, but I paid the price with two of me fingers.

ROBERT *shows* MARTIN *his deformed arm and fingers.*

I were bleedin' all over the floor, and the blood were mixing with the cotton dust. It were like a field of red snow.

MARTIN. Once I were working too slowly up the chimney and Master Brindley lights a fire underneath me. Sure made me work quicker. I was dislodging so much soot that it was falling all over me and filling me pockets and getting me wedged. I was calling and begging Brindley to put the fire out, but he were asleep in the yard. The heat melted me three toes together afore a housemaid heard me screaming and fetched a bucket of water and threw it on the flames.

MARTIN *shows* ROBERT *his deformed toes.*

Now he doesn't light a fire but strips me naked and sends another boy up behind me with pins to prick the soles of me feet. (*Showing the soles of his feet.*) See? And me buttocks.

MARTIN *attempts to remove his trousers to show* ROBERT *his buttocks.*

ROBERT. S'all right, I believe you. I believe you.

MARTIN *smiles, thinking he's won the competition.*

A few pins, eh? You should consider yourself lucky. To punish me for losing me toes, the master put a nail through me ear. (*Offering his ear for inspection.*)

MARTIN *draws near.*

What happened to your eye?

MARTIN. Oh, I forgot. Once the master sent me up a chimney to get a stuck bird. It were a pigeon. Me mother says pigeons are just rats with wings. But this one were small, and delicate, and so frightened. She kept flying towards the light but her wings were so heavy with soot. I tried to take hold of her, gentle as I could, but she took fright and clawed at me forehead. She nearly took me eye. I couldn't see for a blood blister the size of a conker.

ROBERT. What happened to the bird?

MARTIN *stands and prepares to leave.*

Sorry, I weren't trying to upset yer –

MARTIN. I weren't trying to hurt 'er. And I weren't trying to steal 'em spoons. I earn my money. I been up them chimneys since I were six. That's four years. Every time me mother sees me come home with a coin in me hand she cries – big pearl-like tears hanging off 'er eyelashes. Every Sunday we eat meat, and I know I earned my share.

ROBERT. I weren't trying to –

MARTIN. Why do I need to explain meself? For all I know, you
made the whole thing up. I bet yer just a serving boy who
slept his whole life in a bed with feather pillows, serving
jelly with silver teaspoons to rich folk in fine houses.

MARTIN *makes to leave.*

ROBERT. When I were five me father sold me to the mill as a
pauper apprentice. He told me I'd be transformed into a
gentleman. He told me I'd eat roast beef and Yorkshire
pudding. He told me I'd have money stuffed deep into me
pockets. Me first meal was cold milk-porridge of a very
green complexion and me first night I had me first beating
'cause I wouldn't stop crying. When I crushed me arm I was
no use to the master no more. He would've turned me out,
but as it happened the landowner passed away and his son,
Sir Jaffrey, inherited the estate. There were a slave who
worked here. He were released according to the landowner's
wishes, so they were in need of an errand boy. So here I am.
Upon me honour that's the truth.

MARTIN. I believe yer.

ROBERT. I believe yer weren't trying to steal a spoon.

They smile at one another.

You best get back.

MARTIN *turns to leave; he hesitates.*

MARTIN. I know thieving is a sin. But just one silver spoon
and I need never climb another chimney again.

The boys look at one another. MARTIN *jumps from the
wardrobe;* ROBERT *follows close after.*

Scene Nine

A boys' Catholic boarding school attached to an Abbey and run by Benedictine monks, England, 11th November 1888. Singing choristers or similar sounds of the time and place could be used to set the scene.

The papers are awash with stories of a series of gruesome murders that have terrorised Whitechapel in London since the summer. TOM, ARCHIE, HUGO *and* JAMES *are students of the school. They huddle together in the wardrobe.* TOM *reads from a copy of* The London Times *dated 10th November 1888; he reads with flourish. He reads by the light of a church candle or candle-lamp.* HUGO *scratches his initials into the wall with a knife.*

TOM (*reading*). 'During the early hours of yesterday morning another murder of a most revolting and fiendish character took place in Spitalfields. This is the seventh which has occurred in this immediate neighbourhood, and the character of the mutilations leaves very little doubt that the murderer in this instance is the same person who has committed the previous ones.'

HUGO. I thought there were only four.

JAMES. Shhh!

TOM. 'The scene of this last crime is at Number 26 Dorset Street, which is about two hundred yards distant from 35 Hanbury Street, where the unfortunate woman, Mary Ann Nicholls, was so foully murdered.'

ARCHIE. Hugo, what are you doing?

HUGO. Writing my initials. Next to these ones. A–R. Who do we know with the initials A–R?

JAMES (*to* TOM). Get on with it, Tom.

TOM (*reading*). 'About one o'clock yesterday morning a person living in the court opposite to the room occupied by the woman heard her singing the song "Sweet Violets".'

ARCHIE *sings the song 'Sweet Violets', chorus by Joseph Emmet, taken from his 1882 play* Fritz Among the Gypsies.

ARCHIE (*singing the song*).
Sweet violets, sweeter than all the roses...

JAMES (*speaking over* ARCHIE*'s singing*). Shhh! Tom, finish reading it.

ARCHIE (*continuing*).
Covered all over from head to toe.

JAMES. Tom?

TOM *and* ARCHIE.
Covered all over with sweet violets.

ARCHIE (*singing*).
There once was a farmer who took a young miss
In the back of the barn where he gave her a...

TOM.
Lecture on horses and chickens and eggs
And told her that she had such beautiful...

HUGO.
Manners that suited a girl of her charms
A girl that he wanted to take in his...

TOM.
Washing and ironing and then if she did
They would get married and raise lots of...

ARCHIE/TOM/HUGO (*deliberately taunting* JAMES).
Sweet violets, sweeter than all the roses,
Covered all over from head to toe,
Covered all over with sweet violets...!

JAMES (*snatching the paper from* TOM). Well, if you won't read it, I will.

HUGO *snatches the paper from* JAMES; ARCHIE *snatches it from* HUGO *and returns it to* TOM. *They all laugh at* JAMES.

Just read it, would you?

ARCHIE. Somebody's hungry for all the gory details!

TOM. Maybe he's wondering what the papers are saying about him? If you can sneak out of the dormitory to come here, perhaps you can also sneak off to London.

JAMES. Don't be ridiculous. Just get on with it.

TOM. All right. (*Smoothing the paper, deliberately taking his time. Reading.*) 'At a quarter to eleven yesterday morning, as the woman was thirty-five shillings in arrears with her rent, Mr M'Carthy sent an employee to Number Thirteen to get some rent. But knocking on the door, he was unable to obtain an answer. He then turned the handle of the door and found it was locked. A pane of glass in one of the windows was broken. He put his hand through the aperture and – '

ARCHIE (*shaking JAMES suddenly*). Boo!

JAMES lets out a little cry of shock. They laugh at him.

JAMES. You're such an infant, Archie.

ARCHIE. You're the one screeching like a little girl.

TOM. Did you think it was the ghost?

The others make ghostly noises.

They say she was strangled to death.

ARCHIE. In this very wardrobe.

HUGO. By a Royalist soldier during the Bolton Massacre of 1644.

TOM. They say she begged for life. (*Imitating the dying girl.*) Please, please don't kill me.

HUGO and ARCHIE re-enact the strangulation; TOM laughs.

JAMES (*standing to exit*). Fine, if you're going to be like this about it.

TOM (*stopping JAMES*). Wait, wait. No more jokes.

JAMES. Promise?

TOM (*crossing his heart with a finger*). Cross my heart.

TOM *winks at* ARCHIE *as* JAMES *resumes his place;* TOM *continues reading* (*as he progresses through the article his tone sobers*).

(*Reading*.) 'He put his hand inside the aperture and pulled aside the muslin curtain which covered it. On his looking into the room a shocking sight presented itself. He could see a woman lying on the bed entirely naked, covered with blood and apparently dead. Her throat was cut from ear to ear, right down to the spinal column. The ears and nose had been cut clean off. The breasts had also been cleanly cut off and placed on a table, which was by the side of the bed. The stomach and abdomen had been ripped open, while the face was slashed about, so that the features of the poor creature were beyond all recognition. The kidneys and heart had also been removed from the body and placed on the table by the side of the breasts. The liver had likewise been removed and lain on the right thigh. The lower portion of the body and uterus had been cut out and these appeared to be missing. The thighs had been cut. A more horrible or sickening sight could not be imagined.'

Pause.

JAMES. It's him. It has to be.

ARCHIE. But this is so much more...

HUGO. Gruesome.

JAMES. He's evolving. He's developing new techniques.

TOM. Do I detect a hint of excitement, James?

JAMES. No, of course not.

TOM. Do you like the idea of cutting a woman into little pieces?

JAMES. Don't be disgusting. I'm just pointing out that he clearly has a fascination with dissection. Perhaps he's a medical student.

PETER (*mocking* JAMES *by imitating him*). Perhaps he's a medical student.

ARCHIE. Aren't you always reading medical journals?

TOM. James, isn't your father a doctor?

JAMES. Very funny.

TOM. Perhaps they've got it wrong. We shouldn't be calling him Jack the Ripper, but *James* the Ripper!

    ARCHIE *cackles.* JAMES *swipes at him and they play-fight. Suddenly the door handle of the wardrobe turns; they freeze. There is a heavy knock on the door.*

    (*A terrified whisper.*) Father Aloysius.

ARCHIE. No, he's away from the Abbey until tomorrow.

    The knocking on the door grows more aggressive.

HUGO. How did he find us?

JAMES. You were laughing so loudly you gave us away!

TOM (*putting a finger to his lips to silence the others; whispering*). I have the only key.

    A key is heard in the lock. The handle of the door turns.

    (*Imploring the other boys.*) Please don't leave me with him. Please. Please don't leave me with him.

    The door of the wardrobe opens a crack; the room beyond is in darkness. One by one the boys exit the wardrobe: first ARCHIE, *then* HUGO, *then* JAMES.

    (*To* JAMES *as he exits.*) Promise me you won't leave me with him.

    JAMES *nods and crosses his heart with his finger. But as soon as* JAMES *exits, the door is slammed shut behind him sealing* TOM *inside.*

No. No!

The key turns in the lock. TOM *struggles to fit his key in the lock to open it, but in his terror he drops the key with trembling hands. He scrambles on the floor of the wardrobe to find the key before resigning himself to the inevitable, curling his knees up to his chest and hugging them close. He waits. He sings softly.*

Sweet violets, sweeter than all the roses…

Scene Ten

An auction house, an industrial city in Great Britain, 19th June 1916.

A recording of 'It's a Long Way to Tipperary' by John McCormack or similar could be used to set the scene.

World War I has raged throughout Europe since 1914. In January of 1916 a military service bill is introduced providing for the conscription of single men aged eighteen to forty-one. In May, conscription was extended to married men.

NELL opens the door of the wardrobe. She carries a Sotheby's catalogue under her arm. Her fiancé, ANTHONY stands close behind. Beyond them can be heard the sounds of a busy summer English furniture sale. NELL inspects the wardrobe as ANTHONY reads from his own catalogue. The wardrobe is empty.

ANTHONY (*reading*). 'A classic wardrobe of Tudor design with detailed carving including the classic Tudor arch and beautifully panelled doors. Handmade solid mahogany. Believed to have originated in the late 1480s.' (*Looking up from the catalogue.*) That makes it... 1480 to 1917...? Four hundred and thirty years old. I'm surprised it's still standing.

This rouses no response from NELL; she checks the wardrobe meticulously for flaws.

It is believed that it first belonged to Elizabeth of York, daughter of King Edward the Fourth, and mother of King Henry the Eighth, to whom the wardrobe passed on her death. Isn't that astonishing? We are touching what royalty once touched.

NELL. Why would Elizabeth of York ever have touched her wardrobe? With all the servants she had, I bet she never even saw the inside of a wardrobe?

Beat.

(*Reading.*) 'It was lately the property of Downside Abbey in Somerset. The monks used it to house the robes of choirboys. It was purchased from them privately before being professionally restored for resale. It is estimated to fetch a price at auction of – '

ANTHONY *breaks off*.

NELL. How much?

ANTHONY. Didn't you want a painting?

NELL. How much do they say?

ANTHONY. Or what about that Victorian vanity table?

NELL *tries to snatch the catalogue from him, but he whisks it away. She opens her own catalogue and begins to search for the wardrobe;* ANTHONY *stops her.*

Nell, if you want it, it's yours.

NELL. They've done an adequate job of restoring it, I suppose, but there are still signs of wear.

ANTHONY. It's four hundred years old.

NELL. Look at that stain.

ANTHONY. It could be a *royal* stain.

NELL *is not amused.*

Then what about a mirror?

ANTHONY *is about to turn away when* NELL *climbs into the wardrobe.*

Nell...! Nell, I don't think you're allowed inside it.

NELL (*pulling him inside and shutting the doors*). Shhh.

ANTHONY. If we're found in here –

NELL. Anthony, just be quiet.

ANTHONY *falls silent.* NELL *looks around the wardrobe.*

I always wanted a walk-in wardrobe.

ANTHONY. I don't think you're supposed to walk into this one.

NELL. I used to say, 'Ma, one day I'm going to have so many clothes they'll need to custom-build a wardrobe big enough.' 'Fat chance,' she said. 'People like us have two outfits to their name: a set of flannel pyjamas and a serving apron. That's all you'll ever need.'

ANTHONY. Then why on earth are we hunting for antiques? I'll build you a wardrobe.

NELL. I don't want you to build me a wardrobe.

ANTHONY. Then... I don't understand. I'm bending over backwards to buy you the perfect wedding present. And if I didn't know you better I'd call you ungrateful.

NELL. I don't want a wedding present for a wedding I might never have.

Beat.

I know we said we wouldn't talk about it. I thought shopping would help. But it's not working. I think we should go home.

NELL *stands to leave;* ANTHONY *stops her.*

Anthony...

ANTHONY *rifles through the Sotheby's catalogue. Finding what he's looking for, he tears a corner from a page.*

I'm just not in the mood to buy anything.

ANTHONY (*reading*). Eighteen-carat rose-gold Georgian artisan-made wedding band.

He folds the picture of the ring in half and tears a chunk out of the crease so that when he opens it again the ring has a hole in the middle.

Amazing condition for its age. You can still see the hallmarks. No visible wear.

He presents her with the paper ring.

NELL. Anthony…

ANTHONY (*taking her hand*). I, Anthony Edward Leveson-Gower, take you, Ellen Anne Rigby, to be my wedded wife, to have and to hold, for richer for poorer, in sickness and in health from this day forward until death us do part.

ANTHONY *slips the paper ring onto her ring finger.*

Do you, Ellen Anne Rigby, take me, Anthony Edward Leveson-Gower, to be your wedded husband?

NELL *nods.*

You have to say it.

NELL. I, Ellen Anne Rigby, take you, Anthony Edward Leveson-Gower – why do you have to have such a long name? – to be my wedded husband.

ANTHONY. To have and to hold.

NELL. To have and to hold.

ANTHONY. For richer for poorer.

NELL. For richer for poorer.

ANTHONY. In sickness and in health from this day forward.

NELL. In sickness and in health from this day forward.

ANTHONY. Until death us do part.

Beat.

I'm coming back, Nell.

NELL. If you were just a year younger.

ANTHONY (*he's heard this many times before*). Nell…

NELL. If your birthday had been in January –

ANTHONY. Not December, I know.

NELL. Then you wouldn't qualify for conscription.

ANTHONY. Maybe the moment I arrive they'll call a victory. Maybe I'll never see the trenches. And if I do… well, I

won't take any risks or show off or anything like that. I'll
be sensible.

NELL. No you won't.

ANTHONY. Yes I will.

NELL. No, you won't be sensible because you're too bloody…
good. There's nothing you wouldn't do for someone you
cared for. Like going back for a man fallen. Sometimes I
wish you were a bit more of a bastard and put yourself first.

They smile at one another.

Until death us do part, then.

ANTHONY (*smiling with joy*). A marriage isn't legal until
you've signed the register!

ANTHONY *grabs the catalogue and scribbles on the page.
He offers it to her.*

Sign your name, here.

NELL *signs her name.*

Well. I now pronounce us husband and wife.

ANTHONY *tears the signed sheet out of the catalogue and
feeds it through a gap in the wooden boards at the base of
the wardrobe into the secret space underneath.*

I swear upon my honour that I will come back for you, and I
will dig it out we'll take it to the Town Hall and have it
signed officially by the Mayor.

NELL. But how will you know where to find this wardrobe?

ANTHONY. Because we're going to buy it.

NELL. But it's so expensive.

ANTHONY. So what? I might die next week.

NELL (*slapping him on the shoulder*). You can't make jokes
like that.

ANTHONY. Sorry, from now on consider me silent as the dead.

NELL. Anthony!

ATHONY. Come on. This wardrobe isn't going to buy itself!

ANTHONY *exits the wardrobe;* NELL *follows close behind.*

Scene Eleven

Anywhere in the United Kingdom, any time after the publication of The Lion, the Witch and the Wardrobe *by C.S. Lewis in 1950, but before the present day.*

Music relevant to the time and place could be used to set the scene.

A *leads* B *into the wardrobe.* B *shows some signs of being ill, perhaps (s)he wears a nightgown while* A *wears day clothes, or perhaps (s)he has bandages on her arm, or perhaps (s)he wears a hospital gown.* A *carries a copy of* The Lion, the Witch and the Wardrobe.

The object of this scene is for A *to read to* B *from the first chapter of the book while at the same time trying to recreate for* B *the experience as described by C.S. Lewis of Lucy's first adventure into the wardrobe.*

I suggest you begin at the moment in Chapter One when Lucy first steps into the wardrobe. A *reads the relevant lines from the text while ushering* B *into the wardrobe.* B *is initially reluctant and resentful. (S)he interrupts occasionally with protests similar to 'This is so childish,' or 'I can't believe you're making me do this.' However,* A *insists and they carry on and* A *encourages* B *to read aloud Lucy's lines of dialogue whenever they occur in order to give her the full 'Lucy experience'. As they continue, it becomes clear that* A *has planted props within the wardrobe.*

A *prises open a board in the base of the wardrobe and rummages around underneath for props – for example, a fur hat to represent the fur coats; scrunched newspaper or polystyrene peanuts underfoot to create the sound of crunching snow; a fir branch to brush against* B*'s hand; a sieve of icing sugar shaken overhead to recreate falling snow, etc.*

At one point, A *retrieves the signed catalogue page hidden down there by Anthony in the previous scene.*

A (*reading from the catalogue page*). Anthony Edward Leveson-Gower... Ellen Anne Rig... Rig...

B. Rigby.

A. How do you know that name?

B. Ellen Rigby is my – (*Insert appropriate relation depending on how long it's been since the previous scene.*)

A. Who's Edward Leveson-Gower?

B. No idea...

A *tosses the catalogue sheet aside and continues. I suggest that* A *read through the text to the point at which Lucy steps out of the wardrobe into Narnia and feels the snow falling from the sky. At this point,* A *opens her/his satchel and attempts to set the scene of Narnia using household props. Please improvise the lines as necessary, but in a similar vein to the following:*

A. See... imagine this is the lamp post where she meets... and this is the White Witch and this is... (*Revealing a stuffed toy.*) Well, I expect you can imagine who this is. And me, I'm... (*Throwing a scarf around his neck, collecting an umbrella.*) I'm Mr Tumnus.

B *is lost for words.*

It's okay... don't cry.

A *reads the relevant line from the book about Lucy feeling frightened yet inquisitive.* B *nods in response to this.* A *has won her/him over. They smile at each other and continue to read.*

Scene Twelve

A museum, somewhere in Britain, 2014.

Music relevant to the time and place could be used to set the scene.

The doors to the wardrobe opens and FRIEND ONE *enters. (S)he sits on the floor, takes out her/his phone and begins playing a game. The light of the phone illuminates the wardrobe. The door opens and* FRIEND TWO *pokes his/her head inside.*

FRIEND TWO. I knew it was you – what are you doing? You can't be in there, get out.

> FRIEND ONE *ignores her/him.* FRIEND TWO *climbs into the wardrobe and closes the door.*

> You know this is probably alarmed.

> FRIEND ONE *ignores* FRIEND TWO.

> Are we going to talk about this?

> FRIEND ONE *ignores* FRIEND TWO.

> Hello?

FRIEND ONE. Talk about what?

FRIEND TWO. Er, we're in a wardrobe. In a museum.

> FRIEND ONE *concentrates on her/his phone.*

> We have to meet back at the gift shop in fifteen minutes. We're supposed to do the worksheet by then.

FRIEND ONE. I'm doing the worksheet.

FRIEND TWO. This is a wardrobe – it's not on the worksheet.

FRIEND ONE. Yes it is: Question Nine.

FRIEND TWO (*reading from the worksheet*). 'Identify an antique dating from the Tudor dynasty.'

FRIEND ONE. Identified.

FRIEND TWO. Well, we're not supposed to get inside it.

FRIEND ONE. We're investigating the primary source. A historian has to be thorough.

FRIEND TWO. What about the other questions?

FRIEND ONE. Google 'em.

FRIEND TWO. Look, I can't get another detention.

FRIEND ONE. Then go, no one's asking you to stay.

> FRIEND TWO *hesitates*. FRIEND ONE *resumes playing the game on her/his phone*.

FRIEND TWO. Are you all right?

FRIEND ONE. Huh?

FRIEND TWO. Are you okay?

FRIEND ONE. Am I okay?

FRIEND TWO. Yes.

FRIEND ONE. Yeah, I'm fine. I thought you were going?

FRIEND TWO. Nobody's talking about it any more.

FRIEND ONE. If you're gonna go, then go.

FRIEND TWO. I'm just telling you that nobody's talking about it.

FRIEND ONE. Do I look like I care?

FRIEND TWO. Well, you're hiding in a –

FRIEND ONE. I'm not hiding. You think I'm hiding? I don't care what (s)he's saying about me. I don't care what anyone's saying about me. They can say what they like; they can say I'm in to horses for all I care. Horses, goats, sheep, whatever – it's boring. Haven't they got anything better to talk about? So don't even think about going out there and saying I'm hiding.

FRIEND TWO. I'm not going to.

FRIEND ONE. I just can't be bothered with it, that's all. All that whispering and sniggering. It's so immature.

FRIEND TWO. Yeah, I know.

FRIEND ONE. I can't deal with how fake it is; (s)he's so fake. Don't you think?

FRIEND TWO. Well, I –

FRIEND ONE. I wish (s)he'd just be honest about it. Don't try telling me it was an accident. (S)he knew that picture was in there; (s)he knew what (s)he was doing when (s)he uploaded it. So just come out and say it. You want to make a point. You want to post pictures of me on Facebook. Just come out and say it. That'd be so much better. I'd have so much more respect for her/him if (s)he just came out and said it to my face.

FRIEND TWO. I don't think that many people saw it.

FRIEND ONE. I don't care about the photo, whatever, it's just a photo – it's the dishonesty I don't like. I don't have time for that. That's why I'm in here.

FRIEND TWO. Back in the closet?

Beat.

Sorry, I didn't mean –

FRIEND ONE. You know the thing that really pisses me off, yeah? Is that (s)he's trying to make out like (s)he's done me a favour. Like (s)he's helped me by telling everyone for me. As if I wouldn't rather tell them myself. So now (s)he comes out of it looking, like, decent, while I look like I've been lying. Because the fact is, yeah, the fact is I've never actually lied about it because nobody ever actually asked me. You all sit in the same class as me every day and nobody actually asked me, because if they did I would've said, yes, I am. And so is (s)he. And yes we are. And so what? So. What.

FRIEND TWO. (S)he took it down; it's not up there any more.

FRIEND ONE. My cousin saw it. She told my aunt, and then my aunt told my mum and then my mum told my dad and then...

FRIEND TWO. Oh...

FRIEND ONE. It's fine, it's not a problem, it's just...

FRIEND TWO. I didn't know.

FRIEND ONE *can't help it, the emotion bubbles up and (s)he cries.*

FRIEND ONE. It's just... my dad... he just... he looked at me like... I was... some kind of dirty... like he was disgusted or something... I'm fine... I'm fine... I'm not upset, I'm just angry... it's just so annoying...

FRIEND TWO. Hey... look, your dad will –

FRIEND ONE (*tracing her/his finger over the inscribed initials on the wall*). It doesn't matter.

FRIEND TWO. He can't be angry with you for ever.

FRIEND ONE. A–R... H–T... who d'you think wrote that?

FRIEND ONE *takes a key (or similar) out of her/his pocket and is about to add her/his initials.*

FRIEND TWO (*stopping her/him*). No, don't. You can't: this is like a... famous antique.

FRIEND ONE. A–R... Arthur Rex? H–T... Henry Tudor?

FRIEND TWO. Don't be ridiculous.

FRIEND ONE. It could be.

FRIEND TWO. Stop touching it. It's bad enough that we're standing in here. Hey... I'm not saying we should leave. If you wanna stay, we can stay.

FRIEND ONE. I don't care.

FRIEND TWO. Let's just sit in here and do the worksheet. Yeah?

FRIEND ONE *shrugs*.

Come on then. (*Taking out the worksheet and reading*.)
'Question Ten. Identify the spinning mule from the exhibit
"Children of the Revolution".' What's a spinning mule?

FRIEND ONE *searches the internet on her/his phone*.

FRIEND ONE. Spinning... mule... here we go: 'The spinning
mule is a machine used to spin cotton and other fibres. Mules
were worked in pairs by a minder usually with the help of
two child labourers.'

FRIEND TWO (*making a note on the worksheet*). Identified.

FRIEND ONE. I don't get why everyone's making such a big
thing about it.

FRIEND TWO. The spinning mule?

FRIEND ONE. Shut up. About me.

FRIEND TWO. S'just school. People need something to talk
about.

FRIEND ONE. Yeah, but not... this.

FRIEND. Especially this.

FRIEND ONE. It shoun't matter.

FRIEND TWO. Well, maybe one day it won't.

FRIEND ONE. When?

FRIEND TWO. I don't know. Soon. And when that time comes,
d'you want to be the only one who can't – (*Reading*.)
'Describe how the 1833 Factory Act finally changed working
conditions for children'?

FRIEND ONE (*searching the internet*). 1833... Factory...
Act...

*The lights fade on the friends huddled together on the floor
of the wardrobe.*

Epilogue

A museum, Britain, 2014, a few moments later.

The wardrobe rotates so that we once more see it from the front. It is cordoned off by a red rope strung between two brass stands. Next to the wardrobe stands a placard with a detailed description of the exhibition piece.

A group of SCHOOL CHILDREN *file past making lots of noise – chatting, telling jokes, pushing and shoving. A few of them stop opposite the wardrobe to read the placard and fill in a box on their worksheets. One among them calls the others away to see something much better offstage. They abandon the wardrobe and exit.*

The End.

Other Plays for Young People to Perform from Nick Hern Books

Original Plays

100
Christopher Heimann,
Neil Monaghan, Diene Petterle

13
Mike Bartlett

BLOOD AND ICE
Liz Lochhead

BOYS
Ella Hickson

BUNNY
Jack Thorne

BURYING YOUR BROTHER IN THE
    PAVEMENT
Jack Thorne

CHRISTMAS IS MILES AWAY
Chloë Moss

COCKROACH
Sam Holcroft

DISCO PIGS
Enda Walsh

EIGHT
Ella Hickson

GIRLS LIKE THAT
Evan Placey

HOW TO DISAPPEAR COMPLETELY
    AND NEVER BE FOUND
Fin Kennedy

I CAUGHT CRABS IN WALBERSWICK
Joel Horwood

KINDERTRANSPORT
Diane Samuels

MOGADISHU
Vivienne Franzmann

MOTH
Declan Greene

THE MYSTAE
Nick Whitby

OVERSPILL
Ali Taylor

PRONOUN
Evan Placey

SAME
Deborah Bruce

THERE IS A WAR
Tom Basden

THE URBAN GIRL'S GUIDE TO
    CAMPING AND OTHER PLAYS
Fin Kennedy

Adaptations

ANIMAL FARM
Ian Wooldridge
Adapted from George Orwell

ARABIAN NIGHTS
Dominic Cooke

BEAUTY AND THE BEAST
Laurence Boswell

CORAM BOY
Helen Edmundson
Adapted from Jamila Gavin

DAVID COPPERFIELD
Alastair Cording
Adapted from Charles Dickens

GREAT EXPECTATIONS
Nick Ormerod and Declan Donnellan
Adapted from Charles Dickens

HIS DARK MATERIALS
Nicholas Wright
Adapted from Philip Pullman

THE JUNGLE BOOK
Stuart Paterson
Adapted from Rudyard Kipling

KENSUKE'S KINGDOM
Stuart Paterson
Adapted from Michael Morpurgo

KES
Lawrence Till
Adapted from Barry Hines

NOUGHTS & CROSSES
Dominic Cooke
Adapted from Malorie Blackman

THE RAILWAY CHILDREN
Mike Kenny
Adapted from E. Nesbit

SWALLOWS AND AMAZONS
Helen Edmundson and Neil Hannon
Adapted from Arthur Ransome

TO SIR, WITH LOVE
Ayub Khan-Din
Adapted from E.R Braithwaite

TREASURE ISLAND
Stuart Paterson
Adapted from Robert Louis Stevenson

WENDY & PETER PAN
Ella Hickson
Adapted from J.M. Barrie

THE WOLVES OF WILLOUGHBY
    CHASE
Russ Tunney
Adapted from Joan Aiken

For more information on plays to perform visit
www.nickhernbooks.co.uk/plays-to-perform